AUTOBIOGRAPHY

AUTOBIOGRAPHY

Adrian Henri

Jonathan Cape Thirty Bedford Square London

FIRST PUBLISHED 1971
© 1971 BY ADRIAN HENRI

Jonathan Cape Ltd, 30 Bedford Square, London W C 1

ISBN 0 224 00625 8

Printed and bound in Great Britain by
Richard Clay (The Chaucer Press) Ltd, Bungay, Suffolk

The book covers the years 1932–64. I have made it a research project into the person I was at each stage, using old photographs, letters, notebooks and unpublished poems, from which a number of words and images were taken. The last section refers to last summer and might perhaps have been intercut with the earlier sections. I found I could not say anything fresh about my life 1964–70, possibly because it is already too well-documented in existing published work.

I should like to thank the Arts Council of Great Britain for commissioning the 'childhood' section of this book (poems 1–15) for the City of London Festival 1970, Edward Lucie-Smith for constant advice and encouragement, and Jacki Field for deciphering my handwriting and patiently typing the finished work.

Liverpool   A.H.
March 1971

IN MEMORIAM

Albert Johnson   d. May 13th, 1970
Frances Johnson, née Potter   d. May 16th, 1970
Emma Henri, née Johnson   d. June 3rd, 1970
Arthur Maurice Henri   d. June 29th, 1970

I

knocking on the nextdoor door. knocking. no answer. knocking.
on their door. knocking. no answer. silence. then the sound of
something moving slowly painfully inside bumping into things.
door slowly opens. dirty matted hair darkshadowed crusted eyes
wild growth of white hair and beard.

'who are you, then?'
the old twinkle in his redrimmed eyes
'come in, stranger'
he moves slowly ahead hobbling on brokenslippered feet between
objects too shrouded with dirt to be identified
'it's Adrian, love'
'who?'
'Adrian, your grandson, come to see you'
room dark everything covered in soot sunlight barely able to get
through the window. a small fire burning in the grate despite the
heat of the day. she sits there like some terrible white vegetable
unmoving there in her armchair: blind, unable to move, barely
able to hear. sometimes she speaks, then dozes off again. her
hands move occasionally twitch at the blanket round her waist.
the Elsan bucket next to her dominates all the other smells in the
overheated room. the only things in her life now: being lifted on
to it, being lifted off it. sleeping. sometimes speaking to make sure
you're still alive that the other one's still there. a nurse has come
to dress his feet. she peels off the bandages. huge swollen sores
on his poor twisted feet, feet that have been good for a lifetime of
walking, working on a farm as a boy, working for the Corporation
in the park across the road, pushing her in a wheelchair already
semi-invalid for ten miles when they're on holiday. he seems to
doze away, as well, between sentences.
yes, they're all right. just a bit tired today.
no, I can't do anything. the girl from round the corner looks in of
a morning to see if we need any messages.

money? no we're all right.
we've got plenty of food.
space cleared on the oilcloth at the front of the table; all kinds of
tins and packets and old cakes pushed back, disappearing in the
dirt and cobwebs and shadows at the back. finally, helpless, I get
up to go
'all right, son, it's been nice seeing you. it does her good you
know.
come and see us again.
don't leave it so long, next time.
he's going now, love'
'what?'
'he's going now'
'oh, goodbye, love. Tata'
bend over to kiss her. then struggle down the filthy littered
unfamiliar corridor I know from childhood. out into daylight.
grass growing between the cracked pavingstones. two days later
they were taken to hospital. a week later he died. three days after
that she died. I go to look at him in the funeral parlour. face
white, strangely peaceful but they've shaved his moustache off
along with the overgrown hair. why? it isn't him. why can't they
leave him alone? his flesh is waxy, unreal, slight reddish purple
contusions here and there like on a newly plucked turkey at
Christmas. white satin fringed with purple tucked round him.
floral tributes with little cards in Cellophane packed heaped
round his coffin.

Part One   1932–51

1

flags and bright funnels of ships
walking with my mother over the Seven Bridges
and being carried home too tired
frightened of the siren on the ferryboat
or running down the platform on the Underground
being taken over the river to see the big shops at Christmas
the road up the hill from the noisy dockyard
and the nasty smell from the tannery you didn't like going past
steep road that made your legs tired
up the hill from the Co-op the sweetshop the
                                    blue-and-white-tiled pub
Grandad's allotment on the lefthand side
behind the railings curved at the top
cobblestone path up the middle to the park
orderly rows of bean canes   a fire burning   sweetpeas tied up on
                                                    strings
up to Our House
echoing flagyard entry between the two rows of houses
brick buttresses like lumps of cheese against the backyard walls
your feet clang and echo on the flags as you run the last few yards
pulling your woolly gloves off
shouting to show Grandad what you've just been bought
him at the door tall like the firtree in the park
darkblue suit gleaming black boots shiny silver watch chain
striped shirt no collar on but always a collarstud
heavy grey curled moustache that tickles when he picks you up to
                                                    kiss you
sometimes shouting angry frightening you
till you see the laughter in his countryman's blue eyes

11

2

round redbrick doorway
yellow soapstone step cleaned twice a week
rich darkred linopattern in the polished lobby
front room with lace runners and a piano that you only go in on
                                                        Sundays
or when someone comes to tea
Uncle Bill asleep in his chair coming in smelling of beer and horses
limping with the funny leg he got in the war
Grandma always in a flowered apron
the big green-and-red parrot frightening you with his sudden
                                                        screeches
the two little round enamelled houses on either side of the fireplace
big turquoise flowered vase in the middle
the grate shining blackleaded cooking smell from the oven next to it

big black sooty kettle singing on the hob
fireirons in the hearth
foghorns and hooters
looking out of the kitchen window
seeing the boats on the bright river
and the cranes from the dockyards

3

coming back the taxidriver doesn't know where the street is
the allotments at the foot of the hill
gone now
great gaunt terraces of flats
scarred with graffiti
instead
the redbrick houses tiny falling apart
the whitewashed backyard
where you could smell lilyofthevalley through the privethedge
                                                        round the tiny garden
on your way to the lavatory at the end
empty dirty overgrown now
backdoor banging in the wind

grandmother grandfather both dead in hospital
one windowpane broken dirty lace curtain flapping in the wind
the funny little flights of steps
the secret passages in the park
pink sandstone steps overhung with trees up the side of the hill
overgrown or demolished
the big seacaptain's house where I used to go for a present every
Christmas
forgotten
remembering
lying in bed
in the dark crying listening to my mother and father argue
wind banging a shutter
indoors somewhere
dead eyes looking out from flyblown photographs
empty mirrors reflecting the silence

4

RHYL SANDS:
your vision swept clear and bright by the wind that's wiping
away the stormclouds
beach low and empty   pale blue sky   seagulls and one dog near
the horizon
pebbles underfoot as clear as the wallpaper in seaside cafés
somewhere out at sea, a rainbow
the sad peeling offseason colours of arcades and kiosks
David Cox's 'Rhyl Sands' a tiny gem burning quietly in dirty
Manchester
ghostly echoes of last season's chip-papers in the drifting sand

5

the house I lived in destroyed
now a glaring plateglass motorshowroom
only morning glories left on the fence by The Cut
narrow brickwall gorge
a thin trickle of smelly water now

13

not the raging torrent I once fell into coming home crying
                                              covered in pondweed
long low home violet slate roof two front doors with circular
                                              coloured windows
two garden paths big rockery border the rocks painted with
                                              orange spots
(I never found out why)
long rambling garden at the back with the woodyard behind
tall metal fence always coming down
whitewashed outside toilet for my lonely fantasies
echoing flagstone floor to the diningroom my mother said was
                                              haunted
rambling rosecovered fences lilactrees gooseberry bushes
appletree with a black cat climbing in it
Trigger the Wonderdog died aged thirteen in our new Council
                                              House
the old stone houses next door gone
the caravan full of noisy children
the ponies in the field across the road
the sound of donkeys distant in the brickyard field
the rusty whitewashed corrugated fence goals or wickets
by our backdoor where I used to play
gone
now
only a bald concrete patch
outside the brightlit nightglass windows

6

carrying my gasmask to school every day
buying savings stamps
remembering my National Registration Number
(ZMGM/136/3 see I can *still* remember it)
avoiding Careless Talk Digging for Victory
looking for German spies everywhere
Oh yes, I did my bit for my country that long dark winter,
me and Winston and one or two others,
wearing my tin hat whenever possible
singing 'Hang out the Washing on the Siegfried Line'

14

aircraft-recognition charts pinned to my bedroom wall
the smell of paint on toy soldiers
doing paintings of Spitfires and Hurricanes, Lancasters and
Halifaxes
always with a Heinkel or a Messerschmitt plunging helplessly into
the sea in the background
pink light in the sky from Liverpool burning 50 miles away
the thunder of daylight flying fortresses high overhead shaking the
elderberry-tree
bright barrageballoons flying over the docks
morning curve of the bay seen from the park on the hill
after coming out of the air raid shelter
listening for the 'All Clear' siren
listening to Vera Lynn Dorothy Lamour Allen Jones and The
Andrew Sisters
clutching my father's hand tripping over the unfamiliar kerb
I walk over every day
in the blackout

7

walking to the spring wood now a muddy buildersyard
footpaths then mysterious trackless intrepid
now suburban bungalowstreets gravel and tarmac
where the churnedup mud horsedung and puddles were
the woods alive with primrose and milkwort
wood-anemone and bright hawthorn
now a haven for gnomes and plastic waterfalls

8

darkgreen mysterious spaces under hedges
nettles along footpaths
to the Old Mill
stinging your legs
rubbing yourself with dock leaves
dog-rose and sweet briar
angelica and fennel
saxifrage starring the hedgerows

9

seeing into the clear water of the stream
the little wooden bridge
the fields rising on either side dusted with buttercups
darkgreen waterweed swaying
bright ripples echoed in gold below
pale brown blue grey pebbles on the pale sandy bed
eels and sticklebacks wriggling black away from your hand

10

lying on my back
listening to creeping insectsounds smelling the grass round me
looking at the sky
perspectives of sound
crickets   birdsong in the woods across the valley
clover ratstails celandines rabbitdroppings
feeling the movement of the earth
through my closed eyelids

11

water foaming and fizzing round your warm body
sudden rush upwards green light everywhere
sharp salty taste in your mouth your nose stinging
down again gasping your breath in
sounds rushing in cries of bathers distant children
the promenade the Pavilion bright like a postcard

12

sunlight on long grass
old lace curtains draped over raspberry canes
plump gooseberries cobwebbed in the shadows
the smell of lilac and woodfires burning
remembering the day I walked five miles to draw the waterfall

then found my pen was empty and bought a postcard with my
last sixpence
and had to walk home
the postcard still pinned on my studio wall
frozen water falling white blood from a giant's side
walking after cocoa and buns and hearing of a poet's death on the
radio
alone in the vast sad hospital
cowparsley patterning the hedges
light spilt like paint through the leaves

13

deep rosepetals on a close-cropt lawn
the scent of clover lying close to the earth
envious of the coolness under the green rosebush
a sad young poet thinking of her eyes the colour of shadows under
the sycamores
shadows and a myriad insects creep in the tangled grasses
in the evening sunlight
filled with the sound of a thousand departing motorcoaches

14

remembering
the sudden pangs at corners
glimpsing the laughter of happy couples in the street
flat moonbranch shadows on the pavement
under a summer moon
or winter lamplight
nightwalks through the purgatory of half-built housingestates
the last-minute shifting of a cushion
for the seduction-scene that never takes place
for the waiting at the end of the privetlane
for the person who never comes

15
sad
boy-to-be-poet
head full of words
understood by no one
walking the dog
through the midnight bungaloworld
built over the
countryside
of his dreams

Poem for Hugh MacDiarmid

Dear Chris,
If I could only tell, like you
the kind of poetry I want
I write this though
I barely know you
to say 'hello' to

though I have sat and listened to your song
great long river tumbling and coursing with language
leaping with huge strange unfamiliar boulders
marram-grass in the sandy wasteland
quartz-pebbles on a sloping beach
grey moustache stained yellow at the edges
laughing, drink in hand, eternal darkred tie
(tractors ploughing white phosphates in the springtime earth through
the window)

wanting to plait my song
like you
through the streams and courses of life
to make everyone see
to make everyone know
to change the world

no more poverty
no more dying
no more illness
no more ignorance
'the air curdled with angels'
in the bloodred sunset
over the black islands of your songs.

II

ten child's eyes staring bright at the camera on the Sundaybest settee.

AVRIL   hair in curls from the rags it's rolled up in every night. me running with her pram up and down the sandhills. thin, shy, loving the cats, frightened of the gascooker. new Civil Service life, flat with Sunday dinner for me and Andy in Nottingham.

TONY   the brother I took for long walks coming back proud bearing tiddlers flashing in the murky jamjar the spring lanes not yet converted to buildersyards. hitchiking round Europe laying girls in my spare bedroom tired eyes at the dead morning railwaystation.

CHRISTINE   dark beautiful once bitten by the dog now bringing my nephew to see me laughing splashing in the bath. cheeky always in trouble now a nursingsister in a country hospital.

MICHELLE   brown eyes sunburnt face frilly dress. ponytail teenager dancing at parties kissing on the stairs, married in a little flat high above the busy concrete promenade.

ANDRE   round plump Wimpey face fair hair neatly parted T-shirt patterned with motorcars toy cars and electric roadways patterning the floor now tall buying me pints dancing in discotheques.

me an only lonely child then suddenly a brother. brothers with toy trains bicycles and beer sisters coming to Liverpool for summer dresses or winter popstar concerts. coming home laden with parcels every Christmas. no longer knowing what will surprise them what will please them. Christmas dinner treelights wrappingpaper darkness creeping about with laden stockings making mincepics at 2 a.m. laughing with my mother. long summers of picnics on the beach and home over the humpbacked railwaybridge. new school uniforms we couldn't afford every autumn. spring offensives of whooping cough and measles. always letters from my Mum for money. train tearing me away from my childhood as I write this looking at the full breasts of the girl opposite moving slightly under the pink flowered shirt. September sun on flooded fields. me and André and Tony walking back drunk from the pub after the last funeral weekend. 'Christ, we're orphans' he said, suddenly. we moved on, laughing, empty councilhouse full of memories waiting for us.

Part Two   1951–7

1

young
artstudent
under the bridges of Paris
(where else?)
painting badlypainted picturepostcard paintings
Pont des Arts, St-Germain-l'Auxerrois
sketchbook
corduroy elbows on the Pernod table

2

crystalline manna counterpoints the stars
in the deep puddle
frost on gateposts
iridescent
a heavy Williams shadow plunges
blindly between the fuchsias the acacias and the waiting angels
into No. 20, Mon Repos
watched by the lonely poet
midnight dog pissing in the shadows

3

winter evening trickles cold wetness
down black glass between the curtain and the wall
fearing
the stranger's eyes behind your face
when you look too long in the mirror

4

babyfaced   almost thin   N.H.S. glasses
striped college scarf thrown casually over shoulder
various sets of artistic beards and moustaches
learning to drink
Newcastle Brown, Export and Exhibition
Saturdaynight litany of pubs with Alan from the electric train
falling headfirst down a stone colonnade at a Jazz Band Ball
seeing Orphée and Potemkin
waking drunk at 2 a.m. on the roof of someone's house
loving unhappily a greeneyed girl from a mining town
writing adolescent poems of rejection
for something that was never offered
singing on tables and sometimes under them
slipping on a frozen path   the canvas with her portrait
pierced by the stalks of dead chrysanthemums

5

summer loves on the warm concrete promenade
frenzied knickersoff trouserbutton gropings
in the 78 r.p.m. recordplaying frontroom

6

shadowed circle under a summer oaktree at noon
familiar browncheck dress raised high
seeing the strong brown body fully for the first time
down the lane past the little yellow house
confident hands guiding me into you
melting elastic beautiful unfamiliar
afterwards sensible scrubbing at dampmarks
hurrying home so your parents won't know

7

O that summer of lightblue eyes and strong brown hands
reflected in black glass café tables
brown El Greco feet running down alleyways of trees
in the Botanical Gardens
home to love summer rain happy down our faces
tasting the rain on your laughing mouth
pink gums above your littlegirl milkteeth
spending our summer wages getting pissed on Fridays
over the iron railway footbridge
kissing goodnight at the end of the semidetached avenue
so your father won't see us
hiding like mice down backstreets when his big black car goes past

8

trying to paint
the Pasmore morning world
of City allotments
striped huts abstract against beanpoles
curling tendrils of branches into mist
patterns of green leaves against conservatory windows
zebrastriped trafficsign city
red triangles
grey distances against the bright trafficlights

9

the library for
Eliot Pound the enchanted islands
Kafka   Auden   MacNeice
Sydney Keyes dead before the foreign gate

and for
the beautiful blonde librarian
round blue eyes   pale face   child's mouth
full fleecy pinksweatered body

round thighs
watched
across afternoon tenniscourts
across morning bookshelves

10

coming back
to our café
black-and-white-tile floor
still the frothiest coffee north of Sorrento
not
the afternoon hangout for the Grammarschool in-crowd
anymore
now
full of babies with red faces
and middleaged mothers
I suddenly realize
were at school with me

11

PRESTON:
rain splattering my glasses
splintering the neonsigns
24   schoolteacher
in a provincial town

12

meeting you
dark noisy club   nomoney dates
home to my flat
remembering
the morning park   the distant railway
the long green caverns in the treefilled square
loving you
in the crowded coffeesmell Kardomah

13

working
as so often
in the noisy blaring fairground
cream-and-red stalls
creampainted rollercoaster against darkblue sky
working
this time with you
brightlycoloured balloons bursting
ROLL 'EM UP   ONE OVER TO WIN   ANY PRIZE YOU LIKE
powderblue nylonfur poodles
against the bright red counter
children crying   runny noses
holidaymakers huddled like sheep under plastic raincoats
from the August rainstorms
coaches revving up in the carpark
ON THE RED THIRTY-THREE   ALL THE THREES THIRTY-
                                                    THREE
Frankie Laine Guy Mitchell
loud through the electric nightrides.
lights going out   running with the heavy shutters
pints with Big Jim and Georgie Lee in the closingtime
                                              billiardsroom
fishandchip latenight O'Hara's suppers
concrete promenade still warm under our feet
the long walk home
the Townhall clock and the deserted railwaybridge

14

bright still-lifes
proud yellow lemons red tomatoes
orange-and-white Penguinbooks
blue-and-white mug
painted in the little buildershut I rented
down a lane
furnished with a settee for loving you
an easel for your proud body bright against the yellow walls

down to the Dole on Fridays
fairground closed for the winter
flat red sun   black posts   white seagulls
held whirling
against the darkening sands

15

now
the alleyways and market-gardens
gone
instead huge supermarkets empty as the winter seashore
lone shoppers
circling over bargains like seagulls
greeted only by strangers
in the unfamiliar streets

III

saturday morning. reading the lifestory of Dylan Thomas aged 19.
coffee in a greenflowered mug. smell of red beans boiling
downstairs for Arthur and Carol coming to dinner. my brother
and a new girlfriend coming to share the spare bedroom. Sue
asleep as always in the big brass bed upstairs. me at the morning
desk as always, trying to write something I've been trying to
write since June 3rd, 1970, the day my mother died. Tony ringing
at 7.45 a.m. me rushing out having to see the bankmanager before
getting the train but almost unthinkingly stopping to look for a
black tie putting it in my briefcase. he met me at the station and
told me the news I'd already guessed dark circles round tired
eyes. the last time I saw her in hospital two weeks before, I
thought what a beautiful woman she'd been. looking old, thin,
wrinkled with illness but the fine cheekbones and forehead there
as always. hair bobbed dark against the out-of-focus Florida
background of 1930 photos. a blue crêpe dress with a matching
summercoat. a darkblue dress with coloured circles like
Rowntree's pastilles falling into the distance. not for years the
fur coat she always wanted. winesilk danceshoes with diamanté
heels. all squashed at the back of the fading wardrobe, in a
cardboard box a crushed orangeblossom veil. pushed at the back
behind the cheap dresses for the Football Club or the
Saturdaynight pub. beautiful young mother holding my hand
going for a picnic on the sandhills mysterious to jump off like
Sahara now bulldozed into concrete carparks. quick laughing
crying emotional quick to read telling me proudly she'd read
Ulysses in three days. once-a-year concerts of Beethoven. Blake's
Grand March or selections from Gounod she'd play on the piano
for me. Later there was only the drinking club, dirtyjoke
comedians, the hideous songs from musicals. her bending over
beautiful in the darkness to kiss me coming in from a dance
smelling of perfume and gin-and-lime. alone, sad, watching the
shadows on the ceiling, then loving her watching the rainbows

in her necklace as she leaned over me. middleaged, shortsighted, too much effort to read anymore, loving the children's popsongs but still sometimes listening to Caruso and John McCormack. as the children grew older she surrounded herself by cats ramifying family black grey tabby constantly inbreeding. once I used to write home describing every painting I did, everything I wrote. when did I stop? why? suddenly she no longer knew the reason why I did them, only proud of me for the newspaper articles, the television interviews. her ambition, more than perhaps anything else, made me what I am. by the time my first books were published her sight was too bad for her to read them.

Poem for Liverpool 8

LIVERPOOL 8:
blaze of trumpets from basement recordplayers
loud guitars in the afternoon
knowing every inch of little St Bride St
brightgreen patches of mildew redpurple bricks stained ochre plaster
huge hearts names initials kisses painted on backdoors
tiny shop with a lightbulb in the window
Rodney St pavement stretching to infinity
Italian garden by the priest's house
seen through the barred doorway on Catherine St
pavingstones worn smooth for summer feet
St James Rd my first home in Alan's flat
shaken intolerable by Cathedral bells on Sundays
Falkner Sq. Gardens heaped with red leaves to kick in autumn
shuttered yellowgreen with sunlight
noisy with children's laughter in summer
black willows into cold mist
bushes railings pillowed with snow in winter
Gambier Terrace loud Beatle guitars from the first floor
Sam painting beckoning phantoms hiding behind painted words bright
                                                    colours
in the flooded catfilled basement
pigeons disappearing at eyelevel into the mist
hopscotch-figures vomitstains under my morning feet
Granby St bright bazaars for aubergines and coriander
Blackburne House girls laughing at bus-stops in the afternoon
Blackburne Place redbrick Chirico tower rushing back after love at
                                                    dinnertime
drunk jammed in the tiny bar in The Cracke
drunk in the crowded cutglass Philharmonic
drunk in noisy Jukebox O'Connor's
smiling landlord on the doorstep huge in shirtsleeves and braces

LIVERPOOL 8:
now a wasteland
murdered by planners not German bombers
crossed by empty roads
drunken lintels falling architraves
Georgian pediments peeling above toothless windows
no Mrs Boyne laughing in the Saturdaynight Greek chipshop
the tumbledown graveyard under the Cathedral
where we kissed behind willowtrees
bulldozed into tidy gardens
huge tornup roots of trees
pink sandstone from uprooted walls glittering in pale sunlight
no happy dirtyfaced children
littering the sidestreets
only a distant echo of their laughter
across the bonfire fireengine debris.

Part Three   1957–64

1

warm diagonal red-and-black tiles
fire burning in the deep chimneyplace
whitepainted wooden rockingchair   white walls
big regency-striped settee
winter in the little basement yard outside
her voice singing high piping in the kitchen
Saturdaymorning nowork breakfast
reading the *New Statesman*
flames echoing on the low white ceiling

2

blue-and-white-striped mugs
a small stone with holes in smelling of sulphur
we brought home from a beach one day
pueblo-type ashtray from Woolworth's
the sudden apparition, in red,
of the wife of Pierre Bonnard
on the print framed in the alcove
singlebed mattress waiting upright in the tiny wallcupboard
for my hitchiking friends

3

sharing with you
Bird, Monk or Mingus
Mathis der Maler, Das Lied von der Erde
Little Richard or Muddy Waters for parties
same violin concerto always to go home with
rising upwards beautiful
into the proud cadenza

4

Henry laughing red bearded punning face at parties
climbing the scaffolding on the midnight Cathedral
Don studio floor piled with paint plaster wood
moon landscapes even higher than his paintings
John from America a battered Volkswagen laden with pictures
I met eight years later in a New York bar
Ben from Mayfair exiled to grotty Liverpool
keeping a club for our latenight drunken fantasies

5

Brown   knocking on the 4 a.m. bedroom window
'Psst. It's me,
Brown'
laughing   plaid hitchiking jacket   full of news
frantic letters for leftbehind poems
or soiled pyjamas

6

Hawkins
ironing his still-drunk trousers to go home to wife and
motherinlaw
finding an old clown outfit in the wardrobe
enormous   black   red frills and bobbles
bent over the ironingboard
in the hangover morning

7

on a bus
reading Leopardi, the twisted crookback with the winter's smile
patient broomflower 'upon the shoulder of the arid mountain'
seeing
children filing into school

a young man tweedcoated sadly in the yard, On Duty
wondering
how many exiles to the land of concrete lamposts
the drums and trumpets of success
fading in their ears?

8

still
seeing you on a winter beach
bent forward double from the waist
red jacket black trousers like a wooden soldier
nose tip-tilted
inspecting the sound of barnacles on a lonely post

9

Aldermaston dogs scowling through wire at happy marchers
banners black-and-white against Falcon Field
proud trumpet breaking out over the marching drums
the uphill road   tired legs   feet sore
Joyce and I with the huge wurst sausage
we took every year to eat at roadsides
thrown into horseboxes by grinning policemen on demos

10

now
beginning the time of the infidelities
Carol proud breasts warm everopen mouth
Gail who seduced me in the afternoon newstheatre
Pat
my first schoolgirl love
eating buns on the afternoon ferryboat
carving our names in soft red sandstone
one time encased in plaster
from neck to middle   still feeling your warm body through it

35

clear blue eyes   darkbrown hair
loving you
even when finding your phonenumber
in someone else's poem

11

seeing
my first Yves Klein
blue universes in a tiny artgallery
lumpen Paolozzi monsters
Newman horizonlight
serene dark Rothko
Robbie the Robot
making 'today's homes
so different, so appealing'

12

DEATH OF A BIRD IN THE CITY
screaming white splattered against windscreen
crucified on a nightdoor
black words running
lost girl giving you dead flowers
last night's blood on tomorrow's pavement
smells of icecream and antiseptic hospitals
poems sweets comics foodpackets
sweet little Chuck Berry schoolgirls
goalposts chalked on greybrick walls
'The Night, Beware of that dark door'
dying among bunches of nightblack flowers
painted screaming unheard in the tarmac city

13
in Philip's photograph
your hair

grown from the littleboy cut now
backcombed round
on a tube train

face and body brown
from the everyday sunbathing whitewashed backyard
dark hair longer still
in another photograph

at the bar
in our favourite club
loving
but not making love

14

painting huge canvases of Piccadilly
Guinness Clock MOTHER'S PRIDE
bright garden   yellow flowers   grey buildings
huge hoardings for eggs or cornflakes
DAFFODILS ARE NOT REAL
scrawled defiantly across the middle
or
at jinglebells Bing Crosby brass band Christmas
Dreaming Of
her pale secret face
behind the cardboard Santaclaus and cutout reindeer

15

moving from Falkner Sq.
thrown out finally after so many times
after the first party
back from our last fairground summer
laughing friends pushing the settee on its casters
round the Square
brave new home
in a Canning St attic

IV

I suppose he was a bit of a failure, really. at least in most people's eyes. he ended his working life earning a week what I can earn in a night. my mother was always on at him about money. he'd been a bandleader, a social worker, a jolly uncle in a holiday camp, a dancing instructor. yet he ended his life as a miserably underpaid Civil Service clerk in an Army camp near a small seaside town. he'd written a play, he'd produced plays, he'd run a magazine written by unemployed workers during the Depression, he'd worked tirelessly to help other people. yet because he couldn't really help himself we none of us ever really admitted what we felt about him. it's hard to believe dead people are really dead. the waxwork-yellow face, the purple-tinged ears in the Chapel of Rest wasn't him. the black hair just tinged with grey was a cleverly fitted wig. there were Alexandra roses growing up the redbrick hospital wall outside. my childhood was a border zone where skirmishes, rocket-attacks, dogfights took place daily. no prisoners taken. 'look what your mother's done' 'did you hear what your father said'. a lonely observer, fired on by both sides at once. when the children grew up and they withdrew behind their own lives it was too late for him to stop. he used to complain incessantly, often to himself, shuffling about in the kitchen or the garden, a Cassandra in a shabby blue suit, a Jeremiah with no tribe to listen, a shepherd-boy constantly muttering 'wolf', a forgotten Coriolanus in voluntary exile. still a handsome man even into his sixties, black sleekback 1930s hair always chatting up the prettiest girl at the party. after he died we found a Last Will and Testament amongst his things. the name and address and date were filled in. the rest was left blank.

Poem for summer 1967

I think perhaps the thing I've envied most
is my aunts' easy tears at funerals
crying for someone they hardly know and hadn't seen for years
I can't cry for anyone
not really
tears come readily
at the thought of justice or injustice
when they came and put out our bonfire when I was a child
reading Nicola Sacco's last letter
seeing the triumphant crowd bearing banners into the distance
invading tanks and flowers on bloodstained pavements
heard on the noisy foreign radio
not you dying
but the stupid cheap chords of hymns at funerals
brought the tears to my eyes

Scott McKenzie singing 'San Francisco'
nostalgic now further away than The White Cliffs of Dover
long soft body in her husband's bed
walking to the bank in the nextday hangover rain
crowded noisy party
Tony and I picking nasturtiums for our hair
in the darksmelling summer garden
faraway summer gone for ever
thunderclouds massing   mist on trees   flooded fields through hedges

Canning Street polished floorboards home
sideboard elaborate   brickwashed wall above brass fireplace
bedroom collaged with posters to hide where the rain came in
black cat jumping through skylight on to the bed
polish worn away by so many footsteps
so many different faces on the pillow
painting bright salads

meat oozing red electric in the neonlight
tiny universes of creamcakes
clean white canvas waiting ambiguous
Allen singing washing the morning dishes
Bob Creeley laughing at the cardboard I put in my shoes to keep the
rain out
Sunday morning sunfilled Albert Dock with Jonathan

Kissing warm snuggled like childbed
Kissing autumn eyes welling up in the darkened hallway
Kissing away from your best friend under every secret streetlamp

flat now empty
Joyce two streets away room with dried rushes and butterflies

laths fractured sticking through falling plaster
wet paper flapping
rain dripping monotonous
broken-tiled steps to the peeling doorway.

Part Four   Summer 1970

1

moving
once again
strange new worlds of limegreen carpet
cat not knowing where to sleep unfamiliar
doors banging at night apprehensive
downstairs every morning to the windowdesk
schoolgirls laughing beautiful past at 3.45 p.m. daily
blue-and-white dishes
in the evening kitchen

2

Rites of Spring
celebrated in a bluecarpeted room
looking on to the treefilled square
grey spring sky tangled in my fingers with your blonde hair
running my mouth down your warm wet body
the night we had to climb a ladder to your bedroom

3

wind moving high in the summer trees
blowing away the wasp that's near my hand
a tiny yellowgreen insect walking across the blue lines of this
                                                        paper
poppies in the tall grass
camomile and dead nettles swaying
farmgate open
fields of rye rippling in waves
smell of tar from the newlaid road
bright yellow light behind my closed eyes
last year's leaves blowing in the sunlight

4
you
the Yorkshire Poacher
singing over metal nests
two buttering happy
for breakfast
smelling the toasthaze drifting
between the cooker and the door

5

purple loosestrife at the edge of the bay
sea flat grey into the distance
early blackberry flowering along the marshes
tiny troutbeck streams struggling through boulders
soft green hills divided by blackstone walls

warm young body under crimson sweater
patched blue jeans you washed specially for today
wind blowing towards us from the dark mills at the end of streets
warm mouth warm kisses cold hands cold wind
on the station platform

eating Chinese food afterwards waterchestnut crunching in my
                                                          mouth
remembering crisp white teeth
still feeling your soft body against my chest under my arm
eyes wide amazed at the newness of things
alone on your bike in the 3 a.m. newspaper streets
holding my hand on a summer afternoon
writing poems on your examination papers

flocks of wild geese moving across the lake
loving you in frozen silences of fern and rhododendron
the pathway by the water alive with baby frogs
sharing your wonder at the tiny life jumping to escape
from your cupped hands

6

NORWAY:
parked in the middle of the most beautiful landscape in the world
a green-and-red van with SPORTY FORD painted on it
clear viridian depths of cold rivers
waterfalls veiling the sides of granite mountains
last year's snow unmelted   their sides blotting into the mist
laughing blonde girls picking brightpink flowers
old man waiting between the clock and the bed
white birdwings against green fields
small boats lapping at the fiord's edge
unwanted painting
left in the snow outside the painter's cottage

7

you
dreaming of being a salmon
in a lake of crystal water
the scales and dripping waterbeads
changing into a princess's garments
lightfitting hat crusted with rubies and diamonds
trapped by wicked gnomes
in the long grass
across the field
on the way to find the treasure
in the secret garden

8

your familiar voice
on the telephone
happy to type the poems I write for other people
happy to hold the body I give to other people
welcoming me warm into you
happy to make our onenight home in other people's bedrooms

9

rust-red rowanberries
against the rustred roof
of an old barn
inside the warmsmelling hay stacked into darkness
scrambling through tiny streams
clear to the marble fragments on the bottom
ferns higher than your head
dead goose crucified on a bright green cowfield
sudden blood   ribcage   white feathers scattered
small dog jumping for the wildflowers in my hand
a cowman shouting and whistling
across the valley
evening falling
only a trout jumping to break the yellowgreen silence

10

you
in the foreground
farmyard
feeding the ducks
and ducklings
hens and chickens
3 white geese
about your feet

11

living in all my London homes
from home
brokenbacked bedsettee   tiny bed in Ted's spare room
big basement bed in Windmill Hill
arguing with Christopher in a pub
trying to purify the dialectician of the tribe
afternoon wine in Bernard's shop
summer haunted by breasts and minithighs
remembered eyes among rush-hour faces

12

Hampstead   aeroplane garden morning
6 a.m. pale gold bedroom daylight
curtains of honeysuckle and wisteria
darkgreen figleaves
modestly concealing the sky
delicate pink light through climbing roses
morning birdsong   the noise of beginning traffic
pears falling soundlessly from heavy branches
Sunday kites high in the clear air
trees   grass   lakes laid out neatly for inspection

13

you
as Little Nemo
across the magic bridge to Slumberland
curled up sleeping on a bedsettee
in the Palace of King Morpheus

the Girl from Porlock
calling me downstairs from writing this poem
to watch you laughing lying back
in our new bathroom
house full of treasures
you display proudly from the market every Saturday

14

along the churchyard
rhododendron   magnolia
distant bell
path I walked with her as a child
to her mother's grave
dead redandwhite flowers
lashed by the rain as I write

15

after the empty years between
suddenly given
the literary
lion's share
but who
to share it with?
the lion sleeps
confused, exhausted.
the dark outside echoes to his cries.